TODDLER SLEEP SOLUTIONS

Train Your Toddler To
Go To Bed Happily
And Sleep All Night
(Best For Ages 1-4)

Laura Stewart

First Printing, 2014

ISBN-13: 978-1505675474
ISBN-10: 1505675472

Printed in the United States of America

Table of Contents

Foreword

My twins were almost three when my husband and I managed to sneak in a well-earned skiing vacation. Fortunately my Mom was willing to come and take care of my three preschoolers for a week. Wow!

But as you'll hear in this book, my Mom wasn't a softie. She was tough. Loving and caring, but tough. The home where my sisters and I grew up had an enormous back yard with some old woody plum trees. Long plum tree twigs are rather spiky.

If we were ever in big trouble, Mom's looks could kill and she'd snarl: *"Go down and get a plum stick!"* We knew she meant business. We just did what we were told! To my memory, Mom never carried out her implied threat, but it was enough to put the fear of God into us!

We still rib Mom for being mean to us with threats like *"You stop crying, or I'll give you something to cry for!"* or, if we came inside after hurting ourselves – *"Don't you bleed on the carpet!"*

My own children are grown up now, and they know they were always loved. I made many mistakes and I wasn't as tough as my Mom. As my children grew up, I figured out how to treat them so that they would cooperate without me having to threaten them.

I figured there was no point in getting angry with them – I suffered more than they did. They were doing the best they knew how, even when they deliberately misbehaved. True! Toddlers are testing their boundaries – that's all.

I learnt how to set the limits so that my kids would cooperate and they knew where they stood. My Mom was very clear about her boundaries too. She just did it in a different way. . .

As we left for our vacation, we warned Mom about one of the twins. He often woke up and tip-toed to our bedroom in the middle of the night.

He knew that he would get short shrift from me, so he always went to Dad's side of our bed. I didn't even waken. At some point my husband would eventually take him back to bed.

"Well, he won't get away with that!" Mom huffed. I'd conveniently forgotten about her ability to put the fear of God into us as kids. My little boy was sensitive too. Hmmm . . . you'll hear little snippets about her as you read on . . .

For this book I surveyed dozens of mothers with toddlers. The slant is from a parent's perspective.

I'm not a pediatrician and don't profess to be a professional expert. However, I undertook considerable research and have attempted to offer you a quality summary of major findings and first hand experiences.

My aim is firstly to help you understand why your toddler might be having problems around sleep.

Secondly we will discuss factors and philosophies that will help you prevent poor bedtime habits and to train your toddler to self soothe.

Thirdly we summarize and review the main methods used for dealing with sleep problems proposed by pediatricians and various experts in the field of toddler sleep.

For the sake of gender equality, the terms 'he' and 'she' will be used alternately by chapter throughout this publication.

Ladies before Gentlemen.

Introduction

It's Not Turning Out As You Expected

I don't know about you, but when I was pregnant, I psyched myself up - expecting six, maybe twelve months of disturbed sleep – then all would be back to normal. Well it didn't quite turn out that way for me, and I'm guessing that you're reading this book because it's not turning out quite like that for you, either.

As you know, I had twins, so I had NO idea of what to expect! Fortunately I had a supportive husband. Nevertheless, instead of just running a short-term sprint, I found that two years down the track I was still sweating through a marathon.

I'll tell you. There are some options in this book that I wouldn't have the patience to implement. I inherited some of my mother's tough traits. However, what I **did** do, was have a consistent bedtime routine and my husband and I had similar philosophies on discipline – thank goodness!

My twins slept through the night from about nine months old, but there were definitely times when I wish I had known then what I know now.

I would understand more about consistency and patience for a start. Develop those traits and they'll be your best friends.

Like me, you might have enjoyed days, weeks, or even months when your little one actually slept between 7pm and 6-7am, but now, for some reason the rubber has hit the road.

While my twins were toddlers, if it wasn't one, it was the other - especially during teething times.

You tuck your toddler into bed with a hug and a kiss, looking forward to an evening in peace. It's been a long day. The kitchen isn't finished, your partner has paperwork to do, there's a load of washing waiting and you haven't put your feet up all day.

But no, instead of catching up on chores and relaxing, spending some precious time with your partner or watching TV, you're in and out of your child's room, cajoling her to go to sleep. She finally settles - three or so hours later.

Can you relate?

You'd be surprised at just how many of your fellow parents face the same scenario night after night. Even when you turn in yourself, you're still on edge because you just don't know if you'll be woken up in the middle of the night – or why.

If you are currently having trouble with your toddler - either going to bed or awakening during the night, you need to accept that getting her into a peaceful and regular sleep routine won't necessarily be easy. At times when teething, illness or family stress hits it could well be a case of two steps forward, one step back.

We're not perfect and we may have inadvertently set up unhelpful habits already, but take heart – you can reverse them. It may be a gradual process, but in small steps and with patience you can do it.

1

Understanding Toddler Sleep

Of course we all want to sleep well - whether we're adults, children or babies (yes, it's true!) Just as a disturbed night's sleep is difficult for us adults to handle, it is even harder on a young child whose natural sleep routine doesn't fully settle until he's about five years old.

Parental consistency, a united front and patience form the foundation of healthy sleep habits for toddlers. Feeding schedules, social schedules and light (daytime/ night time) all contribute to our sleep patterns. When those three factors are consistent in your toddler's life, you will find his sleep habits are more likely to be as well.

You won't find an "off the shelf" solution to your toddler's individual sleep problems in this or any specific book. You'll need to consider all the different factors contributing to your particular problem and come up with a solution that both you and your partner can agree upon and stick with.

The ability to sleep is a learned skill

Every situation is different – just as every child is. However, it's possible and really important that you train your child to sleep well. Dr. Rafael Pelayo, Director of Pediatric Sleep Service at the University of Stanford has this to say:

"Toddlers physically grow during sleep. Studies show that a human's growth hormone is the highest in the night. In fact, by 30 months, toddlers have gained about four times their birth weight, grown an average 2 to 2 ½ inches per year and acquired most of their baby teeth." [1]

We all know that biologically we need our sleep, but we need to recognize that the ability to sleep is a learned skill. If you want your toddler to sleep through the night without calling for you, it is important that he learns to soothe himself back to sleep because he WILL awaken a few times during the night

The sleep cycle

We all go through cycles as we sleep. The time spent going through the deep (quiet) and light (active or REM) stages of sleep is called the "sleep-wake cycle".

Between each sleep-wake cycle, we all rouse/awaken briefly then re-settle to sleep as we move through the cycles. However until children are about 4, they are likely to wake up more often than we do because their sleep-wake cycle is shorter than an adult's.

A toddler's cycle only lasts about 70 to 80 minutes on average[2]. Toddlers are also more easily disturbed from sleep because they spend more time in the light REM phase of sleep than we do.

Sleep associations

When you are sleeping away from home, have you ever woken up in the middle of the night feeling disoriented and needing to wake up enough to remember where you are? We're used to our own bed and the layout of our room.

What is your normal bedtime routine? Do you have a "must do" wind down activity such as reading? These associations around bed and sleep are embedded in our consciousness. We may have trouble falling asleep if we haven't gone through our "wind down" ritual.

Your toddler is no different. A major key to settled sleep for your toddler is for him to go to sleep the same way that he will wake up in the middle of the night so that he isn't disoriented and nothing has changed.

However, if you always held your baby in your arms as he fell asleep at night, don't be surprised if he resists the idea of going to sleep alone in a big crib. The same goes for rocking or even staying by his side until he falls asleep. This might be fine in the early days, but now, even just your presence while your toddler falls asleep can be his new crutch. When he awakens in the dark and you're not there, it's not surprising that he becomes upset. Where are you?

Many experts suggest that toddlers shouldn't become dependent upon external conditions such as music, lighting, a bottle or a feed at bedtime. My Mom certainly didn't!

However, most mothers I spoke with found that these things just do the trick and they are confident that they'll be able to naturally wean their child when they are a little older.

Some questions for you to consider [3]

- Firstly, have you and your partner discussed your child rearing philosophy? Do you agree?
- If you have different points of view, how do you intend to effectively deal with your toddler's sleep issues?
- How stressful are your daytime commitments?
- How do you both feel emotionally about your child's sleep problems?
- Does your work life require a rigid schedule or are you able to be reasonably flexible?
- What about other lifestyle factors? Do either you or your partner travel a lot?
- What support systems are in place? Do you have other family living close by?

- Is this a good time for you to be considering making major changes to your toddler's sleep routine?
- Can you accept the fact that changing established sleep habits will take time and patience?
- What other factors might contribute to you or your partner's ability to cope with sleep-disturbed nights?

It may be worthwhile to write down your answers.

2

Why Won't Your Toddler Sleep?
Here are 14 reasons

Are you finding that your toddler doesn't sleep as well now as she did when she was a baby?

It just so happens that a wakeful toddler is quite normal. Although not a recent study, the National Sleep Foundation's 2004 Sleep in America Poll[4] found that about 30% of toddlers wake one or more times during the night and as many as 70% of toddlers wake during the night at least once a week.

The reason that you're having issues at the moment is likely due to any of a myriad of factors, both developmental and otherwise. Every child is different; some will sleep more and some will sleep less. Daytime routines, health, stress in the home and your child's temperament all play a role in your toddler's sleep habits.

Once infants turn one, they develop so fast that parents have trouble keeping up – and the toddlers themselves even more so. They are realizing their autonomy and are testing their boundaries. It might be more accurate to say "testing YOUR boundaries", just to see how far they can push you. Being difficult at bedtime is just one way they can try it on.

Depending on your toddler's temperament and the strength of any painful habits, you may have trouble retraining your toddler to soothe herself to sleep. But just like any habit – the longer you wait, the harder it is likely to be to break.

Every toddler is unique. Some will be more energetic and need less sleep. Others may sleep longer, even though they have a quieter disposition. Don't expect your child to have the same energy or stamina as others the same age.

Sleep issues are just as likely to be behavioral as they are physical. Here are some factors that you may not have considered. There are probably many more, too.

Separation anxiety

Separation anxiety generally peaks between 18 months and two years. As mentioned in Chapter 1, your toddler has shorter sleep cycles than we do and is more likely to awaken during the night. It can be scary to be alone in the dark without you. You are your child's most important source of care. If she doesn't want you out of her sight during the day, it's not surprising that she has is fearful when she awakens alone at night.

Environmental factors

Because toddlers are notorious for kicking their bedclothes off, many parents tend to use too much bedding, worrying that their little one might get cold.

More often it is the other way round. Are you sure that your toddler is comfortable and that her clothing isn't too tight or prickly? (particularly labels)

Socialization

From 12 months old, your toddler is more communicative and of course wants to be with you. She can see activity in the household and doesn't want to miss out. For this reason, it is a good idea to ensure the area of the house where she is at bedtime has a quiet atmosphere. We discuss this in more detail later.

Speedy development

During this phase, because toddlers are developing so fast, their little brain simply becomes overloaded. Can you relate to feeling stressed due to brain overload?

For many there is a huge language explosion and you may suddenly have a real chatterbox on your hands. Their awareness is increasing with their mobility and it's not surprising that they want to test out their newfound independence – no matter what time of the day (or night) it is.

Learning to walk, run and jump is not only physically tiring, but can be emotionally exhausting too.

Irregular bedtimes

An ongoing study of 10,230 British schoolchildren has found that irregular bedtimes actually result in worse behavior than going to bed too late.[5] Although the study refers to school age children, the findings would apply even more so to toddlers. A regular bedtime is super important for toddlers' fast developing bodies.

Changed schedules

Your toddler is likely to be more restless during the night when routines change. For example, when she changes from a crib to a bed or when a new baby arrives on the scene - even with daylight saving ... don't expect her to adapt just like that.

These are the times when you may need to employ more skill and patience, still keeping to your normal 'going to bed' routine as closely as possible. Understand that your toddler will take a few days – maybe even a week to adjust to changes in their routine.

An over-active day

If your toddler has had a busy, exciting or social day she may not settle as easily and her sleep may well be affected.

After days like this, still do your best to keep to your normal bedtime routine. Especially focus on calming her down so that she doesn't carry that high energy to bed.

Need for attention

In my previous book "Toddler Parenting", I emphasized the importance of providing your toddler with quality attention. If your toddler doesn't feel loved and important every day, this is very likely to affect her sleeping habits.

Stress in the home

Your toddler is likely to be more aware of tension in the home than you give her credit for. Toddlers pick up vibes – so if you are angry or arguing, don't be surprised if she is also restless during the night.

Daytime nap

This may sound too obvious, but if your toddler had a good sleep in the car on the way home from a long day or she had a late afternoon nap, be aware that she is more likely to resist going to bed. It doesn't hurt to put bedtime back just occasionally.

Imagination

Your toddler is still learning to differentiate fantasy from reality. Before bedtime, it is important to maintain a quiet and calm atmosphere and not arouse her imagination too much. Violent TV cartoons, iPad games or even stories with baddies and monsters are not really appropriate at this time of the day.

Such arousal could easily result in fear of the dark or nightmares. Instead, read a gentle, "happily ever after" story to help settle your little one's vivid imagination before bed.

Illness or teething

It is harder to stick to a consistent routine if your toddler is sick or teething. Of course you'll give her more attention than normal. The problem begins when she gets better and thinks that she can still expect the same sort of attention during the night and/or a different bedtime routine. Try to get back to your regular routine ASAP, both before and during sleep time.

Overtiredness

If your toddler has had a couple of disturbed nights already or some big days without a regular naptime, it's quite possible that she's irritable or demanding because she has become overtired. Overtired toddlers often get a sudden burst of energy just when you are expecting them to wind down.

Other overtired cues to be aware of are hyperactive, argumentative, whiny, or clingy behaviors. Try putting your toddler to bed early for a few nights and watch for tired cues during the day so you might sneak in an extra daytime nap.

Hunger

Your toddler should not be hungry during the night after 9-12 months. If you believe that she cannot last 12 hours without food, try to give her more to eat during the day. From 12 months of age, milk becomes a beverage, not a meal.

If you are still breastfeeding, work on weaning her off nighttime feeds - a small breast feed at bedtime serves as a comfort factor – but that's all.

My Mom was horrified that I was still giving my twins a bedtime breastfeed after they were 12 months old! She still reminds me of how "embarrassing" it was! ☹

3

The All Important Bedtime Routine

As mentioned in chapter two, we all have some sort of bedtime routine. We are unlikely to jump into bed and fall straight asleep after actively doing housework or working on the computer. We probably treat ourselves to a wind-down activity and have some sort of ritual before we turn out the light.

The same goes for your children. It's wise to begin a bedtime a ritual before your toddler has reached 12 months, but if you haven't done so, now is the time. Toddlers love routine and ritual – even though you may not recognize it in them. A bedtime routine facilitates a wind-down period and ensures that your toddler's physical needs are met.

Your goal with your toddler now is to train him to soothe himself to sleep. Follow a regular nightly bedtime routine (bath, teeth, story and bed, for example) so he knows what's expected of him and what to expect during night. The quicker he knows and accepts the ritual, the easier life will be all round.

It is important to keep the evening routine as consistent as possible. When kids are out of their routine they are more likely to act up. Just because your toddler goes to bed late, it doesn't mean that he will necessarily sleep in later. You might be dealing with days of irritable behavior until he catches up.

Look for "Tired" cues

Although you probably want to keep bedtime within a ninety minute timeframe between say 6.30pm and 8pm, you'll experience less resistance at bedtime if you respond to the early signs of tiredness.

Here are some for starters:

- Eye rubbing
- Yawning
- Slowed activity
- Listlessness
- Limpness
- Staring blankly into space
- Whining and/or fussing
- Loss of interest in people or toys

An example routine

There is no "one size fits all" when it comes to bedtime routines. Your child is strongly influenced by his environment, daily activities and other routines.

Your routine will be unique, but it should be predictable.

A regular bedtime ritual including a wind-down period helps your child recognize and establish good sleep patterns.

Your routine might go like this:

- Dinner
- Choosing a couple of bedtime stories (together as he gets older)
- Bath time and pajamas
- Teeth cleaning
- Saying goodnight to other family members
- Turning certain house lights down or off
- Story and cuddle time
- Lights out with door open enough to let some light in
- Tuck into bed with love, as you say a gentle yet firm "Ni-night"
- Leaving the room promptly

Whatever the routine you choose, your aim is to reinforce that certain steps always lead to bed. Start training your toddler at dinnertime by reciting the ritual on a regular basis at first. Tell him all the steps that will happen. Then talk about each next step as you go.

Although bath time might be a good time for giggles and fun, make each subsequent step a quieter one. Whatever routine you settle into, your toddler will pick up on the cues and learn what to expect. You may well find that he likes ritual so much that you'll be reprimanded if you miss a step!

It's important that both/all carers agree on and consistently keep to the same bedtime routine. Both parents should put your toddler to bed at a similar time and have a consistent response to acting out behavior such as stalling tactics and/or grumbling.

It's no good if Mom always puts little one to bed regularly around 7pm after bath, teeth and story, then on the night Mom goes to the gym, Dad allows him to watch TV until he becomes cantankerous. If you both agree in principle, your toddler will know where he stands and this discourages frustrating bedtime antics.

As your toddler gets older, bedtime is a good opportunity for some special 'me time' where you can snuggle next to each other on the bed and remember the day. It's your opportunity to acknowledge good behavior and recount fun times. This one-on-one time is important, especially if there are siblings in the home.

Other points to consider

- It's important that your toddler gets enough active play during the day to help tire him out. Even if it's cold, try to get some fresh air every day.

- Day to day, try to keep meals, snacks and playtime hours consistent.

- Even if Dad comes home close to bedtime, hopefully you can discourage too much roughhousing just before bed.

- Maintain a consistent bedtime routine and don't allow it to become drawn out. Keep the rituals happening and try to keep close to the routine even if upheavals like illness, teething, visitors or a new baby etc. get in the way.

- You'll probably find it easier if your toddler doesn't see the TV going or the iPad lying around as he's getting ready for bed. You won't want to feel like one mother I spoke with. I'll share her story with you in Chapter 5.

- Toddlers don't need milk at night. Limit the amount of liquid for at least 2 hours before bed. If he really needs something to eat, healthy pre-bedtime foods would include complex carbohydrates such as a tiny wholemeal sandwich.

- Don't be tempted to over-dress your toddler in the winter. He is more likely to wake up because he is too hot, rather than the other way round. Using a thermostat controlled heater will help during the cold pre-dawn hours.

- Although you don't want an erratic bedtime, you certainly don't need to have your routine run by the clock. You might have to run a tight ship if both parents are working, but it makes sense that your toddler will sleep better if you respond to his sleep cues rather than the clock. If he woke up late in the afternoon, you might just have to put bedtime back a notch.

- Once your toddler stops his daytime naps, it will become even more important to have a consistent bedtime. If he wakes up at the same time each morning, it obviously makes sense that he needs to go to bed roughly the same time each night.

- For some children, you don't have to necessarily insist that they go to sleep. Your goal may be simply to get them into bed where they might amuse themselves for a while before settling themselves down.

4

Daytime Naps

Average sleep times

This might help you gauge where your toddler lies on the spectrum when it comes to sleep hours.

From 12 to 18 months, toddlers average total sleep of about 12½ hours over a 24-hour period with roughly 10 hours at night and 2½ hours during the day. By the time children are four, this reduces to an average total of 10½ hours a day with less than an hour during the day.

You can expect a young toddler to nap for about an hour in the morning and maybe 90 minutes in the afternoon. Your toddler is ready to move to one nap once she's sleeping consistently at night with 10-11 hours unbroken sleep. If she's is not sleeping right through the night, work on getting that part right before you try to cut down to one nap.

It's important to be observant and aware of your toddler's need for sleep so you can be flexible about daytime naps.

Some toddlers may stop napping at quite a young age and as they get older, only require naps on particularly eventful days, such as after swimming, a play date or some energetic exercise.

Transitioning to one nap

Toddlers generally transition to one nap a day any time from 12 months old. The average age for this transition is 15-18 months. From 18 months, most children have one nap a day until they wean themselves off by about 3½ to 4 years old.

You will get the idea that she's ready to cut back to just one nap if it takes her longer to fall asleep in the morning, or if the morning nap is becoming shorter. Alternatively, her morning sleep may go on for so long that she won't go down for an afternoon nap.

It may be time to cut out your older toddler's daytime nap altogether if she doesn't sleep long enough at night; if it's hard to get her to bed and/or if she awakens too early.

But your child may not be typical. Become aware of the number of hours she sleeps over a 24 hour period and observe the pattern. This way you know what to expect and are more likely to understand irritable or fractious behavior.

Flexibility is the key. It's probably easiest to allow your toddler to make her own natural transition to one nap a day. If she goes to Day Care where one nap is standard, this will certainly have an influence.

If your little one doesn't sleep in the morning, keep a keen watch out for the sleepy cues mentioned in Chapter 3. Be observant and you'll pick up when she's ready for her daytime sleep.

When the daytime naps merge – somewhere around lunchtime, the single sleep is likely to last as long as 2½ hours until your toddler is about 18 months old, gradually reducing to about 90 minutes by three years old.

If you or your toddler are going through an unsettling time, don't attempt to transition to one nap. Make sure you keep to an early bedtime during the change, because if she becomes over tired, you could well have a grumpy toddler on your hands tomorrow. An over-tired and fractious child is also more likely to waken during the night or too early in the morning, thus creating a vicious cycle.

As you go through this transition phase, bear in mind that until 18 months old your toddler may still only comfortably last between four and five hours between sleeps. After 18 months she should still be going to bed within five hours after waking up from her last nap.

By the time she reaches 2½ she may well be able to last up to 7 hours between sleeps.

A naptime ritual

Similar to nighttime, you should establish a naptime ritual. Don't just whisk her away if she is in the middle of an enjoyable activity. This may make the nap feel like it's a punishment.

The daytime routine obviously won't include the same activities as nighttime, but you may still have a feed, provide a bottle or spend a few minutes reading a story. Go in and close the blinds or draw the curtains before you take her into her room. Still say goodnight to other family members or pets around the home. Behave just as you do at nighttime, with a kiss and a cuddle, tucking her in as you lovingly and firmly say "ni-night" and leave the room.

You might find that your toddler doesn't fall straight to sleep, but is obviously happy amusing herself in her crib during naptime – either before or after her sleep. If she's older, she may not even sleep at all, but as long as she's happy she is still having a rest, which is an added bonus for you. If you try insisting that she sleeps, you could be bashing your head against a brick wall.

However, if you know full well that she's grumpy because she's tired and is refusing to go to sleep, you might just have to revert to taking her for a ride in the car or a walk in the buggy. There is little worse than a cantankerous toddler.

My mom recalls that she would simply close the door and go outside to hang the washing – or anything to make sure that she was out of earshot!

5

Prevention is Better Than Cure

Maybe you're one of those lucky parents whose baby really didn't interfere with your peaceful evenings. All he needed was a 10pm feed and he slept through the rest of the night. But then, maybe you're reading this book because for whatever reason, bedtime is now a battle. Once toddlers become mobile, the rules seem to miraculously change. Unfortunately it means you might have to revisit old ground and repeat some sleep training.

If you haven't spent time training your toddler to soothe himself to sleep yet, this may be a longer process than it would otherwise have been.

One overarching guideline for this chapter is that you make a point of NOT waiting until your toddler is asleep or even drowsy before you put him to bed. If you have been staying with him until he falls asleep, now is the time to stop. The longer this habit goes on, the harder it will be to break. We will discuss ways to deal with separation anxiety behavior in the next chapter.

Be observant

If you suspect that your toddler is beginning a difficult new behavior around sleep, the first thing to do is to be alert and maybe even record the trigger points in a journal.

A good idea that many mothers find is to keep a log for a week or so – just so that you can measure how long your toddler is actually sleeping for over a 24-hour period. Record the length of his sleeps and the occurrences when he is unsettled (both day and night). I encourage you to download the bonus worksheets by going to the website at the end of this book.

A smart phone app can also be a very handy tool here. At the time of publishing 'Total Baby' and 'Baby Connect' are the most popular, but they cost. There are free apps as well, which could be worth your research time if you don't want to pay.

By keeping a log, you'll be more aware of whether he's simply objecting to going to bed in the evening or whether you have a consistent middle of the night problem. If he wakes in the night, notice the time and how intensely he cries. At normal wake up times, notice things like his mood - whether he is happy or grumpy. Different situations may have different causes, thus calling for different strategies.

Once you identify the main problem, try to pinpoint the trigger or a pattern. If he is just beginning to resist going to bed, it might signal that it's time to cut out his daytime nap. On the other hand (assuming he is not ill or teething), if he only wakes during the night he might be hot, cold or overtired from a big day, for example. He may be going through a phase of fearing the dark (see Chapter 8). By breaking down the actual problem, at least you know what to work on.

It's not necessarily a problem

Don't automatically assume that you have a problem on your hands if your toddler begins to cry after you leave the room at bedtime or wakes up crying during the night. The less of a fuss you make initially, the less fuss he'll probably make of it too.

Be calm and breathe. As long as your toddler's bedtime routine is consistent, night waking may only be sporadic or at worst right itself within a few weeks.

Before you jump to an assumption that you actually do have a problem and go looking for answers to fix your toddler's behavior, it is worth questioning your own attitude. Spend some time examining your responses to his behavior. You could get some valuable tips from my earlier book "Toddler Parenting". You may find that the problem will pass if you are more consistent, remain patient and deal with his behavior firmly with love.

Eight sleep strategies

Sleep scientists have identified eight sleep strategies that will encourage healthy sleep habits in both babies and young children.[3]

1. Help your toddler understand that nighttime means sleep time. Expose him to outside daylight to reinforce his natural sleep/wake clock (called circadian rhythms).
2. Learn to spot your child's sleep cues.
3. Hopefully you have already established a consistent, predictable and soothing bedtime routine, which will evolve as your toddler becomes older.
4. If your toddler isn't able to fall asleep on his own, now is the time to train him to go to sleep without you having to be in the room. The next chapter focuses on these strategies.
5. Learn to differentiate between normal sleep restlessness and genuine upset crying.
6. Make a priority of daytime naps for as long as your toddler needs it. Children who nap well during the day are more likely to sleep through the night.
7. Recognize that your toddler no longer needs a supper or midnight snack. Train your toddler to use non-food methods to soothe himself to sleep.

8. Remain as calm and as relaxed as possible when dealing with your toddler's sleep issues. Your child always picks up on your stress and is more likely to take that stress on board.

Don't be like my Mom was and make empty threats, either.

Sleep cues

We have already discussed sleep cues in Chapter 3. It might be obvious to you, but many parents get aggravated with their toddler for annoying behavior when in fact they are simply tired. Practise awareness and respond to your toddler's tired signs by introducing a quiet time in preparation for sleep - reducing activities and decreasing stimulation.

Bottles and feeding

Although many experts are critical of toddlers taking a bottle to bed, in reality many of the moms I spoke with use the bottle or a breastfeed as the final settling activity before sleep. Children won't breastfeed forever, so even if you choose not to wean your toddler from a bedtime feed, he will wean himself eventually anyway.

Similarly with a bottle. Toddlers don't need milk or formula at bedtime from 12 months of age, so if he has a feed, work on reducing the length of breastfeeding time, or water his formula down and reduce the quantity over time so that once he is out of nappies at night he has an empty bladder at bedtime.

Use comfort objects for self soothing

There are a number of ways that you can train your toddler to self soothe, apart from relying on a bottle or pacifier. Tender him with a relaxed and affectionate cuddle before you put him into bed. You might give him a gentle back massage and/or stroke his hair.

Encourage your toddler to bond with a soft toy or lovey such as a special teddy or blanket with a soft satin edging. Bonding like this is a sign of healthy emotional development. It encourages independence, helping him deal with separation anxiety and nighttime fears. Loveys can help break emotional attachments to pacifiers and bedtime bottles. You might want to have two loveys so that you can have one in the wash when needed.

My nephew associates going to sleep with his snuggle lovey and lullaby Gloworm (from Amazon) that plays classical lullabies and turns itself off after five minutes or so. He knows how to press Gloworm on and can be heard in the middle of the night using it to soothe himself back to sleep.

Although its nerve racking for parents, it is not uncommon for a normal toddler to sit up and rock back and forth, banging his back and head against the top of the crib to soothe himself to sleep. Don't make an issue of it because you are likely to reinforce the behavior rather than eliminate it. Your little one is likely to stop within ten minutes. Only seek advice from your doctor if the behavior goes on for more than 8 months, if your toddler is well over eighteen months, or if he actually hurts himself.

Anticipating requests

As part of your bedtime routine, consider your child's obvious needs and reasonable requests. Go through the list with him as you prepare for bed... toilet? Teeth? A drink? What stories would he like tonight?

Offer acceptable choices

Since your toddler is testing the limits of his newfound autonomy, it's not surprising that he wants to make more decisions for himself. The trick is to not offer too many choices. "Which story do you want tonight? This one or that one?" On timing, you could show some flexibility by asking, "Do you want to go to bed now or in five minutes?" Your little one still gets to make the choice, but you win no matter which option he picks.

Dealing with FOMO (Fear of missing out)

As your toddler gets older he could easily start to resist going to bed because he sees the TV on or he's in the middle of an iPad game. It's probably worth banning the iPad after dinner and turning off the

TV during the bedtime routine.

Janice was babysitting her two nephews and not being used to boisterous boys, had some hassles cajoling two year old Levi into bed.
He was finally just settling down with the dim lights and the soft lullabies going when in stormed an excited four year old Archie armed with their brightly colored iPad!
"Hey Aunty Jan! Nanna and Pop are on Skype!"
I wanted to throttle him! She laughed.

Listen

You might think it such an obvious word, but in reality, many parents don't listen carefully. There's a saying that goes "It's the space between the notes that makes the music." The same applies when your toddler cries. If you listen carefully, you will work out what he is trying to tell you.

At bedtime, your toddler's cry is quite likely a testing of your limits and not a genuine upset cry – at least initially. This is the time to be strong in your resolve and gently but firmly remind him that it's bedtime. Hopefully he is already familiar with a consistent bedtime routine. If you suspect that there's a good chance of him eventually settling down, try ignoring it and see.

If you DO go into his room, the idea is simply to show that you're here and all is OK. Don't pick him up, but lie him straight back down and repeat the tender "Ni-night, it's bedtime, darling". (your version of course!) Don't talk about anything else and try not to make eye contact.

If he still doesn't settle, wait a little longer before you go in the next time. Repeat the process, but show a more firm and solemn demeanor as you say good night, without making eye contact. You may have to do this a number of times with longer gaps between visits until he gets the message. The length of time you leave him will depend on how distressed your toddler gets and the strength of your resolve.

If your toddler gets too distressed and this strategy doesn't work for you, read onto the next chapter where we discuss other methods of coping.

Older toddlers and stalling tactics

As they get older, toddlers are learning to understand cause and effect, so if you have consistent boundaries around bedtime, your child will know the rules and what is expected of him. If he tries to wheedle for "just one more" story, drink or trip to the toilet, you might allow just one extra request, but make it clear that ONE is the limit.

Stand your ground even if your toddler cries or pleads for an exception. Try not to engage in a power struggle.

Speak calmly and quietly, and insist that when time's up, time's up. Give him one last goodnight kiss; act sort of solemn with minimal talking. Make sure there is nothing else that he can ask for and leave the room promptly.

By paying attention to him - even displeasure - you're reinforcing his behavior. Once your older toddler gets away with being allowed up late for bedtime because you gave in, he is more likely to try that tactic again. Stalling behavior needs to be nipped in the bud.

Older children sometimes become more fearful because they are taking in more of the world around them and are becoming aware of their vulnerability. Never discount or ridicule your child if he is obviously afraid. Instead always acknowledge him for staying in his bed and being "brave". Older toddlers/preschoolers are known to associate sleep with death. We discuss nightmares in Chapter 8.

If you have had to revert to using a stair gate to stop your child coming out of his room, you could use this as a reward/deterrent to entice him to stay in bed: "If you stay in bed, I won't put the gate up, but if you get out of bed, the gate goes up."

To bed or to sleep?

Your older toddler may refuse to lie down to sleep straight away, which could be perfectly OK – particularly if he is sitting peacefully in his bed playing, chattering or looking at a book. Some toddlers are quite happy with their own company, and as long as they're not protesting, they are likely to settle themselves down in their own time.

6

Coping: The Most Popular Models

By the time your baby is twelve months old, hopefully she is used to being put into bed awake. The longer you keep rocking or carrying your toddler until she falls asleep, the harder it will be to train her to settle herself down. As kids get older, they can scream louder too!

At some point in their lives ALL toddlers will test their bedtime boundaries, even those who have been practicing independent sleep for many months. As parents, you need to show confidence, be consistent with your expectations and determined not to waver on your stance.

Don't feel alone if you have a screamer. Apart from reading books such as this, you can also get great support from online parenting forums and Facebook groups.

As mentioned in the last chapter, you need to listen and notice. Pay attention to the type of cry that your toddler is making. If you understand her daytime behaviors, you will be able to better determine if nighttime crying is a try-on or genuine anxiety. It can be a fine balancing act. You need to show that you are there for her by comforting, yet at the same time make a clear point that it is bedtime and you are not far away.

An important caveat at the beginning of this chapter: DON'T try all of these methods. Read through the different approaches, decide which method feels best for you and stick with it. If one doesn't seem to be working, don't simply switch to another midstream! Give it your best shot, otherwise your toddler will become confused and won't know what to expect. An inconsistent response makes it not only harder on yourself – it's even harder for your child.

You might decide to pick the eyes out of the different approaches discussed here and make up your own from a combination of methods. Different approaches are designed to solve different issues - either going to bed or waking in the night.

You might therefore choose two different techniques, depending on the situation. Spend some time observing your toddler's pattern of behavior so that you choose strategies that are the most appropriate both for your child's temperament, the actual situation and your philosophy.

You may have to do some adjusting, so think carefully about your ability to stick with your chosen method. Obviously, your goal is to get your toddler to sleep (or back to sleep in the middle of the night) as fast as you can and avoid her becoming so hysterical that she has no chance of falling asleep easily.

Remember: The more gentle the solution, the longer it will take to get results. No matter what method you use or adjust, be prepared to accept that setbacks will occur.

1. The No Cry Solution

Well known baby care author, Ann Douglas[3] recommends this method if you want to try and get your child to go to bed in the evening without any objection whatsoever.

Temporarily put your toddler's bedtime BACK late enough so that she is actually feeling sleepy. If you have a terror who can stay awake till all hours, examine her overall sleeping routine. You may need to wake her from her daytime nap or begin making lots of noise near her room from 7am if she is still asleep.

As mentioned earlier, toddlers need a certain amount of sleep on average. Keeping a journal for a week or so will alert you to the number of hours she sleeps and possible adjustments you can make.

When you know that she is ready to go to bed without any fuss, go through your standard bedtime routine so that the ritual is linked with sleeping. Now work backwards. Gradually bring her bedtime FORWARD by about 15 minutes a day until you are happy.

This is an easy method to implement if you have a relatively placid child. However, you need to be committed to sticking with the bedtime routine over the long term.

2. Parental Presence

This method may be appropriate if you have never trained your baby to sooth herself to sleep, or she has not been separated from you at sleep time before.[6]

- Go through your normal calming bedtime routine and when you switch off the light begin a quiet activity of your own within sight of your toddler. If she stays awake, quietly whisper that it's sleep time, so that she knows you are in the room. If she becomes distressed, say and do as little as possible to calm her down and go back to what you were doing. Repeat the process until she falls asleep.
- While you wait for her to fall asleep, choose to do something for yourself such as reading (most Kindles and iPads make this possible these days), yoga, using a fit ball, headphones or even ironing (perish the thought!)
- If your toddler is 18 months or older you might try this: Tell her that if she lies quietly, you'll stay with her but if she doesn't stay lying down and go to sleep, you'll leave.

- Keep your promise. In theory if you're consistent you'll break the habit. If not, you may have to revert to the gradual withdrawal approach.

The obvious problem with this method is that you are still not training your toddler to self soothe and she is still associating going to sleep with having you nearby.

3. Gradual Withdrawal

This option helps children who may find self-soothing too difficult for various reasons (e.g. co-sleeping or high levels of separation anxiety[6]). It is also described in a different way by Kim West, The Sleep Lady.[7] You might want to visit either of those sites to get more detailed information.

The gradual withdrawal method takes about two to three weeks to implement. It initially involves using either a mattress on the floor or a chair beside the bed. You'll probably get some sleep yourself if you use a mattress, which of course depends upon your personal situation.

Begin with your normal calming bedtime routine. When you tuck your toddler in, settle yourself down, either lying or sitting so that your toddler can see you. Don't make any eye contact. In fact you could pretend to be asleep. (what a great opportunity for meditation!) If you must respond at all, just repeat a boring phrase like "Its bedtime now, sleep tight". Be there, but remain unavailable.

Stay lying or sitting still until she falls asleep. Keep the mattress or chair close to the crib for about three nights and then move it halfway to the door for the next three nights. Hopefully your toddler is gaining trust that you won't abandon her and is beginning to settle more easily.

Can you imagine my mother doing this? LOL!

By the end of the first week, you should be able to have moved your mattress or chair close to the bedroom door and then after nine or so nights, move the mattress/chair outside her room. If this method has been successful so far, once your mattress or chair is outside the door you are free, but you could still just re-appear every so often. Obviously you would only do this if your toddler hasn't fallen asleep. It reassures her that you're around.

This is a slow and tedious solution to employ. You need patience and determination and your partner needs to be on board to provide support. Unfortunately, you only have to stay by your child's crib for two nights for your presence to become her expectation. Another problem with staying in the room while your toddler falls asleep occurs when she wakes up in the middle of the night. If you're not close by, you're possibly back to square one.

This is not to say that this method won't work. It will IF you have a clear consistent plan. At the end of the day, any of these methods will work if parents consider their strategy carefully and see it through to the end.

4. Controlled Crying/Attended Cry It Out

A number of sleep experts advocate this method as being the most effective and middle of the road – neither too tough for your toddler nor too demanding on you. It can be used both at bedtime and in the middle of the night (as long as it doesn't disturb others in the household). Be prepared to be patient and consistent – possibly spending hours, even whole nights initially.

I will discuss two situations where you may choose to use the controlled crying method:

  a) *Crying or calling from their crib or bed*
  b) *Getting out of bed and coming in to you*

a) *Calling out or crying and screaming*

If you have followed a calming bedtime ritual and your toddler calls you after you've left the room, don't go in immediately. Listen to her noises. Is it a genuine upset cry with tears or is she just fussing loud enough to get your attention? Oftentimes **any** attention (whether positive or negative) sends her a message that fussing gets results.

What if you try not responding for a while? Your toddler may well settle herself down.

If the fussing goes on for a bit - even if the volume is escalating, keep calm and call back to her to reassure her that you're not far away. Remind her that it's bedtime. If she still continues to "cry" or call, keep repeating the same response "It's sleep time, ni-night". Baby monitors are handy in this situation, because she can hear your response without you having to call out.

My Mom recently looked after my 18 month old nephew
while my sister went on a short vacation.
Guess what the first thing she did was?
Turn off all the baby monitor receivers!
"Oh, I can't stand that racket!" she announced.

Do your best to resist going back into the room. This is the way unhealthy habits begin. Assuming that you know she has everything she needs, this type of crying is likely attention seeking. You only have to be tough a few times for her to get the message.

If she starts to get really upset however, go in but don't stay. Just make sure all of her needs are met and lie her straight back down. Give her a gentle, but quick stroke the first time as you say goodnight before leaving the room.

If she continues to cry and you have to go back a second time, leave it a bit longer before you return. Show a firm demeanor and don't make eye contact. Don't get angry or show any exasperation or frustration.

On the other hand, don't reward her by staying, either. Don't touch her or engage in any conversation. Simply lie her back down and reaffirm that it's sleeping time now, saying goodnight as you leave the room.

You may have to repeat the process time and time again – but make the gaps between visits longer and longer (5, 10, 15 then 20 minutes) and every time you go in, make your visit shorter.

You might find that this process takes up hours the first night – particularly if it is in the middle of the night. But at least you are checking on your little one regularly. After a week or so most toddlers get the message that you're not going to give in and will eventually sooth themselves to sleep.

b) Coming out of their room

If your toddler starts coming out of her room, nip that behavior in the bud the very first time it happens. (Remember my mother?) Make a point of telling her that it's not on. Either pick her up or take her by the hand straight back to her bed. Avoid engaging in any conversation or making eye contact with her as you take her back.

Be consistently calm and focused on getting your child back to sleep. Act sternly with downcast eyes and a monotone voice: "It's night-time, now". Make sure she is comfortable and leave the room promptly.

5. Cry It Out (CIO)

If you simply let your toddler cry, she will eventually fall asleep. However studies have shown that there could be health risks associated with this method.[8] You toddler may get so upset that she may even vomit, so you need to listen carefully enough and be aware of what is happening for her. You also need to be positive that there is no genuine reason for the crying, such as a dirty diaper.

Pediatrician Richard Ferber[8] became renowned for his CIO theories. However it appears that he has often been misquoted as suggesting that it is OK to let a baby cry herself to sleep. His method of progressive waiting appears to be more closely aligned to the controlled crying method discussed in point 4.

Some parents feel OK with the cry it out method, which supposedly works within a week or so. Others find that they can't handle the crying long enough to give CIO a chance to work.

Currently there is more of a movement against letting your toddler cry it out – particularly in the middle of the night.

This is a much more scary time for them and more disruptive for you and others in the household.

Leaving her to cry is more likely to result in her becoming hysterical, by which time she has no idea why she is crying anyway. This can be a frightening experience for a toddler and fear is not a good teacher.

Also be aware of your own limitations. If you already find it hard to listen to your toddler scream during a 20 minute tantrum during the day, consider how you would cope with it for possibly a few hours every night over the next week or so.

It's horses for courses. If your toddler doesn't become hysterical easily, it may well be the most appropriate option. You'll need to have a strong resolve and feel optimistic about the outcome, though.

Do your research and have a free week in front of you. Depending on your toddler's temperament, it may be impossible to implement the CIO method on your own, so ensure you have your partner on board or some other close support. Make sure your toddler is not teething or off color at all and keep siblings out of earshot.

If you decide to go through with this, the next few days will very much harder on you than they will be for her. If you are consistent, CIO will work.

Following is an extract from another standpoint:

"Crying is the only way babies have to communicate they are stressed and leaving them in this state only increases their stress levels and teaches them they cannot rely on their caregiver to assist them. A baby left to cry experiences a flood of cortisol (stress hormone) in his body. Repeated extreme stress responses can have an adverse effect on brain development.

Additionally, neurological studies show the pain of emotional separation registers in the same way as physical pain. The pain a baby experiences at being left alone to cry is clearly quite intense.

If a baby is left to cry he may finally fall asleep. When our bodies are flooded with too much stress and the cortisol level increases, the body has no choice but to shut down. It is then flooded with pain numbing chemicals and hormones in an effort to physiologically and emotionally retreat from pain it cannot withstand. This is a highly toxic state to be avoided at all costs and can be damaging for the young babies developing brain.

Stress at this level causes neural cell death and impairs optimal brain development while simultaneously weakening bonding and attachment systems. Babies cannot make sense of a caregiver who is attentive at some times and distant at others."

http://www.parentscentre.org.nz/parenting/sle epandattachment.asp

Older toddlers and consequences

Door shutting

This tactic can result in lots of tears and you might find it too harsh. Certainly don't shut the bedroom door if your toddler is teething or ill in any way. Because shutting a child in is a potentially frightening experience, it could well make matters worse. However this is a method to try if you think it will work in your particular situation.

Since older toddlers understand choices better, you could warn your child that if she gets out of bed, you'll hold the door shut until she goes back. Some parents revert to throwing a towel over the door so that it is hard to open. Stay behind it at first and keep it closed for one minute. If she hasn't returned to bed by then, leave it closed for another two minutes, extending up to five minutes on the first night. Hold no conversation apart from repeating what you are doing and what you want her to do.

Once your toddler gets back into bed on her own, open the door, offer a quiet word of warm acknowledgement, and leave without going inside the room. On subsequent nights, if she keeps up the behavior, gradually increase the time that you leave the door closed – but certainly keep it under 30 minutes.

A much less scary option would be to use a baby gate to keep your child in the room.

Don't be surprised however when you go back a little later, to see your toddler asleep on the floor near the gate!

Reward Systems

A more satisfying and happy way to teach your child about consequences is to offer a reward for her staying in bed and going to sleep on her own. You might use a star chart, or make little "certificates" for her to collect and when she has a certain number, she is allowed to choose a special treat of your choosing.

7

From Crib to Bed

Many parents find that moving their toddler from the crib to a bed solves all of their sleep problems. Their toddler no longer feels trapped and has plenty of room to move now. Generally toddlers graduate to a bed anywhere between 18 months and three years of age. However, there are many factors and it depends upon his size and emotional maturity.

This is an exciting move and an obvious indication that your toddler is growing up and becoming more independent. However, most experts agree that it is best to put this move off for as long as possible. Just the same, if your little one is trying to climb out of his crib or is looking at all cramped, it's probably time to make the move.

There are a number of factors to consider. Firstly, don't make this transition when there are other things going on in your family life such as moving house or if your toddler is going through a phase of waking up during the night. You'll find it much easier if he already goes to bed happily and sleeps through the night.

Especially don't make the move if Mom is more than six months pregnant with a sibling. Apart from a new baby, another inappropriate time is when the baby needs to move into the crib. Some mothers actually find it helpful to leave the empty crib in the room for a little while as their toddler becomes used to his new 'big bed'. Other parents begin by just allowing their toddler to sleep in the bed for daytime naps, before moving to full nights in the big bed.

Make this move exciting for your toddler. Let him be involved (or at least think that he is) in choosing new bed linen. You may feel the need to purchase some bed rails if you fear that he might fall out. Another solution is to put a mattress or some big cushions on the floor next to the bed. Many parents decide on a toddler bed as an interim move. You can even purchase a crib that can be converted all the way into a full size bed.

Your toddler may take a couple of weeks to adjust to sleeping in his new bed. Here are some more tips to make the transition easier. You can adapt his bedtime routine a little now as well.

- Encourage him to climb into bed himself.
- It's nice to pop yourself up on his bed for story time.
- Now he is a little older, use the opportunity to spend just a little more private "me time" with him while you talk about his day and give thanks for all the good things that have happened. This is a great

opportunity for you to let your little one know how proud you are of him in his 'big' bed.

- He'll probably still want his lovey, if he has one. You might also allow him a couple more soft toys now that he has more room around him.
- Continue to offer the same reassuring but firm "Goodnight" when you leave the room. Let him know that you'll see him in the morning.
- Praise your toddler if he stays in bed all night – this really IS a big step.

After the confinement of a crib, you might find that your toddler exercises his independence and gets out of bed after you tuck him in. Your approach shouldn't change from before. Be loving and firm, take him straight back to bed and remind him that it's bedtime now.

If you continue to have problems, re-visit the previous chapter on different coping strategies.

As for my Mom when she looked after my twin toddlers?
The very first night that she heard the pitter-patter of little
feet down the passage, she boomed out in the loudest,
scariest voice, "GET BACK TO BED!"
Instant sleep training!
My son never came into our room during the night again!

8

Night-time Fears

With your toddler developing so fast, she is taking in an enormous amount of information and often doesn't distinguish fantasy from reality. Hence, nighttime fears can raise their ugly head. It is really important to screen any sort of media that your growing toddler is likely to take in – not only at bedtime. Sad stories and spooky pictures might easily remain in your little one's memory because of her heightened imagination.

Fear of the dark and of monsters is quite a normal part of your toddler's development. Sometimes it's easier said than done to train her to cope with those fears, particularly given the threatening shows and games that our children are exposed to these days. It's a case of finding the right balance between acknowledging her fears and over consoling, which may result in you inadvertently reinforcing them.

Some contributing factors

- Separation anxiety tends to peak between 18 months and two years and this is an important factor to consider if your child is fearful. If you think this might be the case, ensure that she receives quality attention during the day.

- Toddlers are more astute than we give them credit for and if your little one has picked up on any stress in the household, this could easily manifest itself in nighttime fears.
- If you're like most parents, you probably allow your toddler TV time. However, it makes sense to prevent her from watching anything scary or violent from mid-afternoon onwards.
- Scrutinize games that your kids play on your tablet as well – particularly after dinnertime. Even if the games are not scary, they can easily trigger an energetic and imaginative mind.
- Be aware of the stories that you choose for bedtime. Always choose gentle, "happily ever after" ones.

Although you don't want to discount your toddler's fears, you don't want to over reassure either. Be light hearted about monsters. They could be silly or funny; they don't have to be scary! Turn the light out as soon as possible after story time. Many parents have a low night-light on in the room, or leave the door ajar with a light on outside until you retire.

If your toddler talks about "scary monsters", use normal waking hours to work on convincing her that they don't exist in real life.

Explain to her that dreams are really just ideas that we have in our sleep. You can do this by playing a little game of 'pretend'. Here's an example: "Lets close our eyes and pretend that we can see an ice cream . . . Can you see an ice cream? . . . OK let's open our eyes now. Is there really an ice cream here?"

Your goal is for your child to feel safe enough to handle anything that might happen through the night. Just the same, it may well be easier said than done to convince her that monsters or other imaginary problems are not real (especially when we expect them to believe in Santa Claus), so here are some tactics that moms I spoke with have employed.

- Put some water in a spray bottle and label the bottle "monster spray". You might even put a tiny bit of coloring in it. Understandably many parents don't like this approach because you are not being truthful and when your toddler finds out, she may well wonder what other untruths you have told her.
- Some parents have reported that their toddlers feel empowered by being able to use the spray themselves, but this tactic may well backfire on you too!
- Use the hand held vacuum cleaner to suck up any monsters that might be lurking in corners or cupboards.

- As long as your toddler isn't sensitive or prone to allergies, you could spray some air freshener in the room and tell her that monsters hate the smell. Your little one will notice the lingering odor as she dozes off.
- Tell her that monsters aren't allowed in your house and they have to stay a long way away.
- Buy a special soft toy that your toddler agrees is the "monster scarer" especially for her room.
- Make a sign for the bedroom door that says "No Monsters Allowed!"

NOTE: It is best not to introduce tactics like this if bedtime fears are only a random or passing occurrence. i.e. don't jump into organizing a spray bottle the first time your toddler mentions monsters. And of course, realize that tactics such as these might actually reinforce the idea of monsters being real.

Nightmares [9]

Nightmares occur during light REM sleep, often during the second half of the night. They become more common after three years old because preschoolers are now more aware of external events in the world around them now. During their sleep they process occurrences that occurred during their day.

As toddlers grow, they also become more aware of their vulnerability when they have unpleasant experiences such as hurting themselves, being bullied or even experiencing some wild weather. Preschoolers are learning to handle their own emotions and label their feelings, so it's good to discuss any scary things that happened during the day soon after Day Care. Don't leave such discussions until bedtime.

If your preschooler awakens because of a bad dream, don't discount her fear. The dream may not be real, but the fear is. The best response is to comfort her with a cuddle and some reassurance that the dream wasn't real.

If bad dreams persist, look for sources of chronic anxiety in your toddler's daily life.

Night Terrors and Confusional Events [10]

Your child could also suffer from night terrors, which are different from nightmares. However, genuine night tremors are quite rare; only about 1% of people actually experience them.

On the other hand, confusional events are more common in children aged from three to six and can range from being quite mild to fairly intense. During a confusional event your toddler may appear to be upset or frightened and can scream inconsolably. She might shout out or even get out of bed and sleepwalk. She may have her eyes open but won't even seem to realize that you are there. She is still asleep and won't remember the occurrence.

Such an experience can be terrifying for you the parent, but there is nothing you can do to stop it. You're unlikely to wake a child in this state – nor would you want to. Just stay with her and continue to offer comfort. Confusional events may last anywhere from two to thirty minutes.

Confusional events are not seizures and not dangerous unless your little one is thrashing about in a way that might hurt her, so ensure that the area around her is clear. You will know when the event is over and your child settles back down. You may decide to consult a pediatrician if these events begin to happen too often for your liking.

True night terrors are very intense confusional events and typically last only between one and five minutes. Both events occur when your child is moving from a deep (non REM) sleep to a lighter phase of sleep (earlier in the night than nightmares), generally about 1-2 hours after falling asleep.

Experts have found that the following factors may contribute:

- Being overtired – the most likely reason
- Having a disrupted sleep schedule or routine
- Sleep disorders such as sleep apnea or restless leg syndrome
- Awareness of a full bladder - this would only apply to confusional events. Parents have reported that

taking their child to the toilet, (even while they are asleep) has ended the event.

- Heredity may play a part, so check to see if others in the family have suffered night terrors – including sleep walking and/or talking.

9

Early Waking and Other Issues

Most toddlers need 12 hours sleep a night on average. However, if you kept a journal for a couple of weeks, you might find that your child only sleeps say, for an average of 10 hours. If he tends to be generally grumpy or not as happy as you would like, it may well be that he is suffering from a lack of sleep.

If your toddler wakes before 6am and didn't go to bed early, it could well be due to overtiredness. Overtired children don't sleep soundly or as long as well rested children. He may be:

- Short of sleep – either going to bed too late or not having a decent daytime nap
- Staying up too long between his afternoon nap and bedtime
- Going to bed overtired, past that sleepy but still awake point. If he is too drowsy going to bed, he will not have learned how to soothe himself to sleep. This would be a real problem if he wakes up too

75

early and doesn't know how to fall back to sleep on his own.

Other reasons for waking up early

- Apart from being overtired, a soggy or dirty diaper may be the problem. Invest in the most super absorbent ones you can.
- Incorrect temperature can also be a key trigger that awakens a toddler. As mentioned earlier, parents tend to over-dress their infants for bed, so be aware if it will be a warm night.
- On the other hand, in winter a thermostat-controlled heater could keep the pre dawn chill at bay.
- Summer sunrise is another obvious reason where block out drapes would be a wise investment.

If your toddler wakes a good hour too early, respond reasonably quickly so that he doesn't wake himself (or you) up too much. Go in, or use the baby monitor and forcefully tell him that it's still nighttime and Mom and Dad are still sleeping.

You don't need to snarl, though!

___

If you have no success, at least convince him to amuse himself in his crib until you come in.

Just as you would do in the evening, you need to insist that he either goes back to sleep or plays quietly.

If it's way to early, have a go at one of the methods recommended in Chapter 6 to get him settle back down. You don't want to become a slave to 5am!

If he's in a bed and comes into you, take his hand and firmly take him straight back to bed, giving him the same message. By this age you could teach him what a 7 looks like. Purchase a picture alarm clock with big numbers and insist that he stay in bed until the 6 or the 7 shows up, or the alarm goes off.

More strategies for early wakers

- You may need to put his bedtime back a bit.
- Tracy Hogg, author of "Baby Whisperer"[11] suggests the idea of waking a young toddler an hour before he normally does and changing his diaper so that he will then sleep to a respectable hour.
- Don't change bedtimes over the weekend.

Sleepwalking

Sleepwalking is not uncommon in children. Up to 15% of young children will sleepwalk at some stage.[12] This phenomenon occurs more when children are deprived of sleep. It therefore makes sense to ensure that your child always goes to bed at a reasonable and regular hour.

Unlike nightmares, sleepwalking occurs during deep sleep. Don't try to restrain or yell at a sleepwalking child. Simply guide him back to bed.

If your toddler sleepwalks more than once, it would probably be a good idea to put an alarm at his bedroom door so that you are alerted. Make sure his room is clear so that he doesn't trip over anything. Keep a nightlight on in the room and put up a safety gate.

Don't talk about his sleepwalking the next day. He won't remember the occurrence. He is likely to feel embarrassed which would only make the problem worse. He may resist sleep because he fears it happening again, resulting in a vicious cycle.

Teething

During these times, you have to allow some leeway. A teething child can feel mighty miserable – especially during the night. There is a plethora of gels and infant painkillers to help relieve the symptoms. You might try some homeopathic teething powder. Vaseline rubbed around your toddler's mouth will help prevent a dribble rash.

Coughs and colds

It is so easy for toddlers to pick up infections from Day Care – or anywhere, really. Again, little children can feel wretched, probably more so than we do because they don't know how to blow their nose until they are about two.

Make sure you keep to a strict bedtime routine, but you'll obviously need to be more responsive, patient and understanding.

For congestion, many parents find that a cool mist humidifier in the room during the night helps. You just need to be pedantic about keeping it clean so that it doesn't blow more germs into the room. These days you can buy humidifiers that don't require expensive filters.

Other simple solutions for a cough include using Vicks Vapor rub on your child's feet and then putting his socks on. You can use infant paracetamol to reduce fever and make sure he has lots of fluids (but not milk) at night.

Habits form quickly

You will obviously need to make allowances while your little one is not well. This is certainly not the time to leave your child to cry for any length of time, even if it is a controlled period.

However, it's also important to bear in mind is that it only takes two or three nights for a habit to form, so if you choose to stay in your toddler's room for longer or take him back to your bed when he is not well, you'll need to be strict about returning to your normal routine as soon as you can once he is better.

Teeth grinding - Bruxism

The *Journal of Dentistry for Children*[13] estimates that about 38% of toddlers grind or clench their teeth at some stage. When it happens in bed it can be quite loud, and your toddler can even wake himself up with the noise! It often occurs when a child is ill from a cough or cold and may stop when he is well again.

Young children grind their teeth mainly because their upper and lower teeth don't sit together comfortably. You really can't do much about it apart from visiting the dentist who may be able to polish the teeth that are rubbing. If you are really concerned, see a paediatrician. Usually this is a short-lived habit and most children will grow out of it by the time they are six.

Does your child wake up alert?

According to Doctor Pelayo[1], children should wake up refreshed. If that's not happening, there may be a bigger problem. Some children suffer from sleep apnea, a sleep disorder characterized by pauses in breathing during the sleep cycle.

Others struggle due to enlarged tonsils because while they are sleeping, their throat muscles relax. Enlarged tonsils can then block the relaxed airways and the child awakens himself to catch his breath. Both of these issues inhibit sleep, causing children to wake up exhausted.

The family paediatrician needs to be notified of any problems with breathing during sleep, including snoring.

Other sleep issues

There is a whole range of disorders that may result in disturbed sleep for toddlers. These include ear infections, gastric reflux, allergies, eczema, autism, dyspraxia, ADHD and other special needs. Discussion of these issues is beyond the scope of this book.

10

The Transition from Co-Sleeping

Depending upon your philosophy, you will probably take a different approach to transitioning your child from sleeping with you to sleeping in their own room. If you are committed to co-sleeping and enjoy the experience, you might make the transition later than if you are simply co-sleeping because it was the easiest solution to nighttime dramas.

However, prevention is better than cure: If co-sleeping is not your chosen philosophy and you don't want your child sleeping with you for months, don't allow the habit to form in the beginning. Use one of the methods spelled out in this book to train your baby to self soothe. Of course there will be times to make special allowances, such as when they are ill, but do your best to get your toddler settling back in her own bed again as soon as possible.

Maybe you once enjoyed having your baby sleep with you but you're now ready to make the transition. Spend some time thinking it through so that you understand your reasons. Your awareness will help you implement the move.

Part of you will mourn the change, so take your time. But don't renege. Make sure you're not making the transition just to appease other peoples' opinions. Ambivalence can defeat your plan, so be confident. It will make for a more peaceful switch.

You can still share your bed is on weekend mornings after everyone has woken up. It can be so much fun for kids to jump into Mom and Dad's bed on a lazy morning. These are the special days when all the family snuggle or sprawl together in bed and share games and cuddles with each other.

Daytime naps

It is better for your toddler not to have her daytime naps in your bed. Have her nap in her own crib or bed – either in your room or her own. At least then, if you choose to switch from night-time co-sleeping, you only have to work on one transition.

Begin the process by training your toddler to enjoy playing in her own room. If it's not happening already, change her daytime naps to her own room for a while before you do the night-time transition. It's a good practice to make her bedroom (even her crib or bed) a special place that she is happy to amuse herself in.

If you're lucky you'll be able to convince your toddler that now that she's a big girl, it is time, to have her own bed in her own room. Initially however, you may choose to allow her to sleep in a separate bed in your room.

Your toddler is quite possibly going to resist the move, so don't expect her to make the transition within one night or even one week. Accept that she is likely to want to return to your bed quite often at the start.

This is an appropriate time to alter some parts of your toddler's bedtime routine, but overall, keep it the same. You might begin by putting pajamas on in her bedroom. Then have story time on her bed. There are other changes you could make, but initially spend a little more time ensuring that all her needs have been met and assuring her that you're not far away, allaying any fears she might have.

When the transition is hard

Every situation is different. If you want the more gentle approach, you might choose to sleep on a mattress in your toddler's room and gradually move it further and further from her bed such as in the Gradual Withdrawal approach discussed in Chapter 6. This of course will take longer than an immediate transition, but for a child who has been used to your presence at night with a lot of attention, it may be kinder to use some form of gradual withdrawal method.

Of course you will achieve quicker results by making a clean break and working on coming back to your toddler's room if she cries – just to assure her and to put her back down to sleep quickly. As discussed in Chapter 6, if your toddler continues to cry, keep going back, but make the gap between visits longer and the time spent in her room shorter.

It's important that you go to your toddler, rather than vice versa. If your little one comes into your room, unless she is teething or ill, swiftly take her back to her own bed. Ensure that she has everything she needs, remind her that it's sleep time and give her a quick "goodnight" without making eye contact.

Even if you have to repeat this process dozens of times, don't get discouraged even though it is really tough. Stick to your guns. If you give in, you're just making it harder for yourself in the long run. According to sleep experts, it only takes three nights of being tough before a habit like this is broken. It could well take longer than that for you, but if you keep calm, say nothing except "it's bedtime/night-time", don't make eye contact and refuse to give in, it won't be long before your toddler is sleeping happily in her own bedroom.

You probably won't know yourself when you have your partner to yourself again. Wriggly sleepers leave and intimacy returns (we hope!)

Conclusion

In the end, to train your toddler to sleep, you really need to just go with the flow. You may still get frustrated, but hopefully you're able to put some of the techniques mentioned in this book into practice so that you can handle the issues in a more relaxed and confident manner.

If you want to enjoy your toddler, do your best to accept that night waking is a normal part of life. If you look at sleep interruptions as a problem, it will be much harder than if you remember that these precious years fly by and these problems won't last.

Just as you probably wake at times during the night, so will your toddler. He just needs to be able to soothe himself back to sleep. This is a skill that he has to learn and it won't happen overnight (pardon the pun). Patience is the key, but remember my Mom. Sometimes you may have to employ some tough love.

KEEP
CALM
AND
CARRY
ON

You are the parents and you are in charge. Your toddler needs leadership in order to feel secure. Don't allow your child to push your buttons.

The end goal for any sleep training, regardless of age, is simply to be able to put your child to bed and leave the room, knowing that you will all have a peaceful night's sleep.

Special Toddler Sleep Bonus

As a bonus to "Toddler Sleep Solutions" you can download a complementary Sleep Journal for your Toddler (yes, the spelling is correct, either way). This is a really practical worksheet that will help you identify any problems and work out the best solutions for your specific situation.

Tailor it to your own needs by making comments as you work through it. You can even make your own pages to fit with your specific timetable.

http://12u4u.com/toddler-sleep-bonus

Other Recommended Reading

Toddler Parenting

The first book in this series.

References

[1] http://www.families.org.au/default.aspx?go=article&aid=834&tid=1

[2] http://www.tresillian.net/tresillian-tips/settling-techniques-12-months-to-toddlers.html

[3] Ann Douglas: - *Sleep Solutions for your Baby, Toddler and Preschooler* (2006)

[4] http://sleepfoundation.org/sleep-polls-data/sleep-in-america-poll/2004-children-and-sleep

[5] http://www.npr.org/blogs/health/2013/10/15/234683175/random-bedtimes-breed-bad-behavior-in-kids

[6] http://www.tresillian.net/tresillian-tips/settling-techniques-12-months-to-toddlers.html

[7] http://sleeplady.com/babysleepsolutions/ (not an affiliate link)

[8] Richard Ferber: *Solve Your Child's Sleep Problems* (Revised 2006, 2013)

[9] http://www.babysleepsite.com/night-terrors-nightmares/

[10] http://www.babysleepsite.com/sleep-training/toddler-preschooler-nightmares-how-to-handle-part-2/

[11] Tracy Hogg: Baby Whisperer: *Sleep: Secrets to Getting Your Baby to Sleep Through the Night. (2009)*

[12] http://www.babycenter.com.au/a558189/toddler-sleep-concerns-sleepwalking

[13] Journal of Dentistry for Children http://www.aapd.org/publications/

Made in the USA
Middletown, DE
30 July 2018